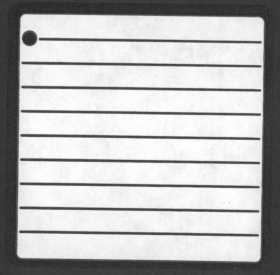

# Money

# and

*A First Book*
*by Lois Cantwell*

# Banking

A GROLIER COMPANY

*Franklin Watts*
*New York • London • Toronto*
*Sydney • 1984*

Photographs courtesy of:
New York Public Library: pp. 4, 12, 17, 19, 24;
Robert Sefcik: pp. 8 (Phillip Davis Collection),
29 (top and bottom), 46, 51;
UPI/Bettmann Archive: pp. 26, 33, 48;
Culver Pictures Inc.: p. 38;
Federal Reserve Bank: p. 42;
Department of the Treasury, United States Secret Service: p. 55.

Library of Congress Cataloging in Publication Data

Cantwell, Lois.
Money and banking.

(A First book)
Bibliography: p.
Includes index.
Summary: Traces the history of money and banking
and discusses such related topics as credit cards,
counterfeiting, and coin collecting.
1. Money—History—Juvenile literature.   2.Money—
United States—History—Juvenile literature.   3. Banks
and banking—History—Juvenile literature.   4. Banks and
banking—United States—History—Juvenile literature.
[1. Money—History.   2. Banks and banking—History]
I. Title.
HG221.5.C27 1984          332.1'09          84-7428
ISBN 0-531-04827-6

# Contents

# Money
## and
### Banking

*To my husband,*
*Robert Sefcik*

# 1    *How Money*
*Started*

We need money for many things. To buy food, pay rent, buy clothes and other goods, and to use services offered by doctors, barbers or music teachers. We donate money to charity and we save it for a new bicycle or record albums. Adults earn their money in many different ways. Mail carriers, teachers, fashion models, and astronauts all earn money. Young people can earn money too. They can receive an allowance for doing chores, they can deliver newspapers, shovel snow, cat sit or mow lawns.

Once there was no money and people bartered or traded for their needs and wants. Money is much easier to use, though, and today hardly anyone barters. If you were going to barter, you would have to bring around all your trading things everytime you needed something you didn't have. And then you'd have to find someone who had what you wanted and was willing to trade for something that you had. That's not a very easy task.

Money started when some members of a community decided to place a value on an object that was small and could be carried around easily. Sometimes the only value that money has is what everyone agrees that it has. So, at different times in history iron nails, shells and even cacao beans were used as money. Salt was used to pay Roman troops in ancient times. The Latin word for salt, salarium, is the basis for our word salary.

It took many centuries for money to develop, even after the first kind of money, coins, arrived on the scene. People tended to use coins along with barter; a loaf of bread and a coin might be traded for shoes. One of the earliest civilizations to work out a form of standard barter was Egypt, dating from about 2500 B.C. Many tomb paintings from ancient pyramids show Egyptians trading. Wooden boxes for shoes and fish for bread were two common types of trades.

In Egypt, as in many places in the ancient world, cattle were treated as a form of money. And standard gold weights were even ox-head shaped. Cattle are not the best kind of money, though. Among other things, their value depended on their weight and health. So your money could get sick and die! They are also expensive to keep, feed and tend, and hard to move from place to place. And it is impossible to make change.

The ancient Egyptians never had any proper coins. This may be because no one in the society really needed to buy anything. All the rich and powerful people already owned everything that they would need and they had many slaves to grow, build or create what they didn't have. Slaves didn't need money, either. They weren't paid for their work and weren't allowed to own anything. There wasn't much of a middle class between these two.

By the year 2000 B.C. the Egyptian culture was beginning to die out. King Hammurabi of Babylonia was the most powerful ruler in the world. He started using grains of wheat as the standard in weighing and measuring gold for buying and selling things. All kinds of financial business took place in the temples of Babylonia, which acted as banks, of a sort, with the priests acting as bankers. Business records about interest on loans and exchange rates, for example, were kept on clay tablets stored there. Some of these tablets can be seen in museums today. But for all of their banking and business dealings, there were no coins, no real money as we know it today.

It took about another thousand years for a civilization to think of the idea of coins. In approximately 650 B.C., Lydia, a small nation in the Mediterranean was a busy city on the trade routes for Egypt, Persia, and Assyria. The idea of having a standard exchange token with a sure value seems to have come from shop-keepers dealing with merchants from many different lands. The very earliest form of coinage may have been invented when a merchant tired of weighing the same lumps of metal over and over. He may have decided to make a mark after he already weighed a lump, showing the lump's value and his name so that he would recognize it if it came his way again. Other people began recognizing certain merchants' marks. A baker may have used an X mark and a tailor a T, for example. Since the people trusted the merchants, they trusted the marks.

It's a simple step to go from marking metal lumps by hand to gathering many lumps and marking them by machine to save time. With these "coins," a Lydian baker could price his bread at three coins (or three lumps) and not have to figure out if an Egyptian gold ring was worth the same as a Persian weight of gold. Some of these Lydian coins exist today. They are made out of drops of a naturally formed mixture of gold and silver called electrum which was mined near and in Lydia. The metal was cleaned and then melted. Drops were poured out to be cooled and once they had cooled down, they were placed on an anvil. A mold was placed over the drop and it was struck with a hammer, leaving a design on one side and the rough anvil marks on the other.

It is not surprising that electrum was used to produce the first coins because gold and silver have always been considered valuable. The metal is beautiful, lightweight, and sturdy. It can be cut up into small pieces of equal value or stamped with an amount— or pictures—of the things it can buy. And amounts of great value can be stored in a small place and hidden during a robbery or war.

At the same time that Lydians began coining money, so did the ancient Chinese. The Chinese had set up value tables showing how many of one thing you could trade for something else; seven jars, for example, would buy one ox.

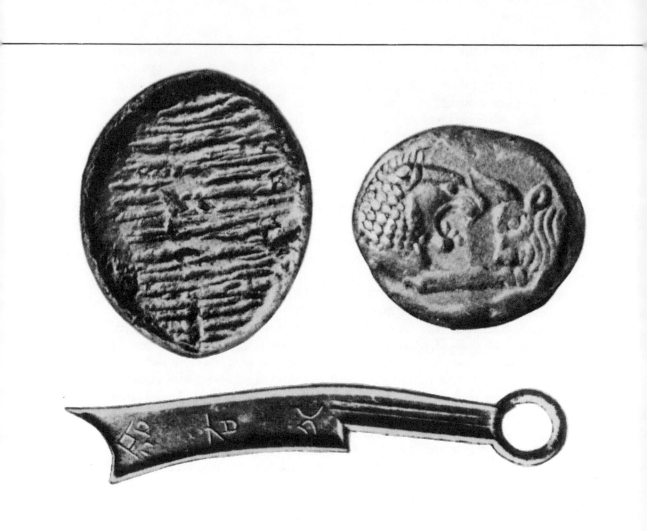

*These coins were among the earliest money.*
*At upper left is a Lydian coin of electrum; at*
*upper right, a later Lydian coin of gold; and*
*at bottom, an example of Chinese knife money.*

The very early Chinese coins resembled farming tools: shovels, or spades. These coins were made of copper, iron or bronze and were engraved with their weight and the name of the community where they were made. Another kind of spade coin, *pu* money, was smaller than the other coins. A third kind of ancient Chinese money was called knife money, after its shape. This kind of coin had a ring at the end so that several coins could be carried together. As time passed, the knife coins became smaller and smaller until only a flat circular disk with a square-shaped hole remained. Coins of this type changed very little over the last 2,000 years. The Chinese people stopped issuing them only in the early twentieth century.

The Lydian coined money was very popular. Lydia's King Croesus was the first ruler ever to guarantee the value of a state's money. He also changed the basic money system from the use of electrum to the production of pure gold and pure silver coins. When he and his country were conquered by the Persian King Cyrus, the Persian people liked the Lydian money system so much, that they gradually stopped using their own money and began using the Lydian's. The idea of coins was then spread by the Persian traders throughout the civilized world.

The ancient Greeks also liked the idea of coining money very much. And they improved on the crude markings of the Lydian and Persian coins making some of the most beautiful coins the world has ever known.

# 2

## Ancient Greek
## and
## Roman Money

ach Greek city-state produced its own coinage with pictures of its own special symbol: from an ear of corn to turtles, owls or lion heads. Greek gods were also pictured on the coins. Each coin became a mini-sculpture, a piece of art that took about two months to make. The Greeks also minted one of the smallest coins in history, the *obol*, which was as small as a pinhead and was often carried around in a person's mouth, so it wouldn't get lost. At least it wouldn't if it wasn't swallowed!

Some of the world's earliest banks were in the temples of Delphi and Delos in ancient Greece. The banks were then supposed to be protected by the Greek gods. One of the most important jobs that these early banks had was changing foreign money to local money for all the traders from many lands who came to Greece. Almost every community made its own money which was only good in their own town. The ancient Greek bankers also accepted money for safekeeping, loaned it out, and charged interest on it.

So, during the Golden Age of ancient Greece, from approximately 400 B.C. to 300 B.C., coins changed from marked blobs of metal into circular, shaped, stamped coins. The Greek coins were made by pouring melted gold or silver into coin molds to make blanks—flat circles of metal with no markings. When the blank cooled enough to be formed, but was still warm enough to easily take on a new shape, it was hammered into a specially prepared die and then put into cold water to cool. The hammering forced the design onto the coin. A die is another kind of coin mold. Since these dies were made of tin and bronze and cracked easily the Greeks invented a way of creating a very strong master die, or hub, to create other dies. This way, coins would remain alike even if a die broke. Mints today still use hubs to make dies.

Coins were a big part of the ancient Greek trade system. There were no credit cards, electronic banking or checks; people could either use coins for trade or resort to barter. Coins were minted in many values. One coin could serve as an entire day's wages instead of a sack of grain or a chicken.

The best Greek coins were made around 500 B.C. in Athens, which was a powerful Greek city-state. One reason that Athens produced the most popular coins was because most Greek coins were made of silver and Athens controlled the silver mines.

But within two hundred years, by the middle of the third century B.C., Greek coinage was almost at an end. By that time much of Greece had been conquered by Alexander the Great of Macedonia and Greek ways of making coins, as well as Greek designs, were slowly forgotten. And as Rome became more powerful, their coins began to set world standards.

The earliest Roman coins date from around the fourth century B.C. They were crude lumps of bronze called *aes rude*; they had no standard weight or value. The next type of coins made by the Romans were the *aes signatum*. These were large five-pound bronze bars, each of which might have a different design such as a bull, eagle, elephant or ear of corn; these may have stood for bartered objects. By about 270 B.C. the *aes graves* appeared. These were also large bronze pieces, but were circular or coin shaped and had a standard value.

All of these kinds of money were made in the same way: by pouring melted bronze into molds and letting it cool. Later Roman coins were struck using the Greek method, which was much quicker and easier. The Romans minted silver and gold coins in the third century B.C. and were the first to introduce ridges around

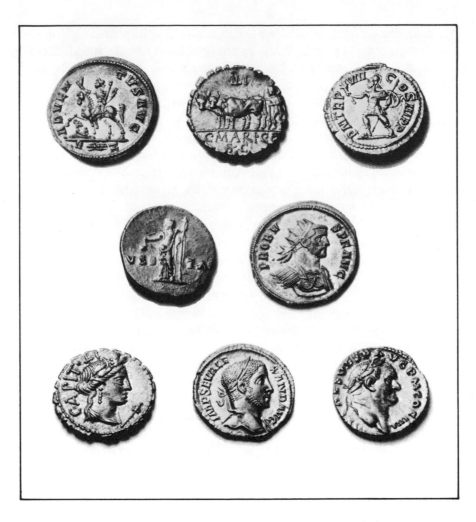

The earliest of these Roman coins (upper left)
bears the likeness of the goddess of the harvest,
Ceres, on its face and a farmer plowing with a
yoke of oxen on the reverse side. The other coins
show Roman emperors on their faces and different
gods and goddesses on the reverse.

the coin edges to prevent clipping or the shaving of metal from around the edges of the coins. They also put designs on the coins, which guaranteed their value and showed where they were made. During the first century, the official Roman mint was located behind the Coliseum in a temple dedicated to the Roman goddess, Juno Moneta. Our modern word, money, is based on her name.

As opposed to the grace and beauty of the Greek coins, Roman coins were sturdy and practical, designed to hold up to heavy circulation in all the corners of the Roman Empire. Most Roman coins were made in the one central location. After the first century A.D., Roman coins carried a kind of list of all the great things that the Roman emperors had done—or said that they had done—for Rome.

A great part of the money for running the Roman Empire came from the profit the rulers made on minting money. So, in order to increase their profit, the amounts of gold and silver in the coins were made smaller and smaller. By the third century A.D., there was practically no gold or silver in the coins at all. This happened at about the same time as the division of the Roman Empire into two parts—the western and eastern empires—and the beginning of the decline and fall of Rome.

# 3

## Money During
## the Middle Ages
## and Renaissance

The western division of the Roman Empire was invaded by Goths from Germany and Huns from Asia. These were savage tribes, much less civilized than the Romans they conquered. These tribes contributed little to a Roman culture that was rapidly declining. For many centuries, the only coins minted were very crude copies of older Roman coins. For the most part, communities either used old coins or bartered. In the eastern part of the empire, or Byzantium, coins were still minted. The best known of these coins was the solidus, a clean gold coin of a standard weight. These coins were very popular and were minted for about 700 years.

The art of coinage was more or less lost in Europe during the middle ages. As in art, science, and literature, all the coins produced were either bad copies of what had been made before or originals of little quality. Coin makers had to reinvent ways of minting which had been forgotten for many years. There wasn't even much of a demand for money because life was based on a society called feudalism. This way of life was not based on trade or commerce, but on land ownership. A lord would give some land to a knight. In return, the knight would promise to fight the lord's enemies. Since the knight *was* usually fighting somewhere or another, his land was farmed and tended to by peasants. The peasants and their families were allowed enough food to live on. The surplus food was taken by the knight, who in turn gave them anything they needed that they could not make themselves. But even so, there were some coins being made during this period.

The first important medieval mint was opened in London about 600 A.D. and two hundred years later an important system of money values was started by Charlemagne. From that time on, a pound of silver would have 240 deniers, or parts. The small "d" stood for penny in England—much the way "¢" is used in America—as late as the 1970s. The "£" of British pounds (the equivalent of our dollar sign) is from the Roman *libra,* meaning weight.

By the time of William the Conqueror (1066) there were almost one hundred mints in various parts of England. The minting procedures were similar to those of the ancient Greeks and Romans. It's hard to believe that over 1,000 years could pass without many changes being made, but it's true.

Around the twelfth century A.D., commerce started again among European nations and coinage increased in Italy, France, and Germany as well as in England. The German coins, bracteates, had designs only on one side and were extremely light, thin, and fragile, but were very beautiful—with pictures of lords in suits of armor, for example.

The Italian coins, called grossos, came from Venice, were much smaller, and made of silver. In the next century the Venetians issued gold coins called ducats; during the same period, gold florins were produced in Florence. The thirteenth century also was the time when Louis IX introduced the first French coins, which weren't known as francs for another hundred years.

One reason we know so much about medieval coins is that anyone who had any money tried to keep it safe by burying it. Modern historians have been lucky to find great numbers of coins which were forgotten by their owners.

During the Renaissance in Italy a brand-new type of coin was invented. Coins were sculpted in wax, then a metal mold was

made from the wax sculpture. Melted metal could be poured into these new molds creating beautiful coins with an unshiny, unhammered finish. A mechanical coin-punching machine which could create blank coins—as well as other machines which would stamp designs on the blanks—were invented around this time, too.

This was the first giant step toward a modern minting system. These machines took the place of men weighing, cutting, and finishing coins by hand. There were also heavy rolling presses to make coin metal into thin sheets, a job which used to take much longer when the metal had to be hammered by hand.

By the sixteenth century, the well-known English coin, the sovereign (20 shillings), was in use, as well as the crown. Both these coins remained in use for many centuries, even though the values changed quite a bit through the years.

Also, during the sixteenth century, commerce between nations expanded. Merchants who traveled from one country to another, however, were afraid of being robbed, since they often carried large amounts of gold with them. In Holland, men called "cashiers" began watching over other people's money for safekeeping, and soon the goldsmiths' guild began offering a similar service. If a merchant would leave his gold and valuables in the care of a Florentine goldsmith, for example, the goldsmith would give him a receipt or letter of credit which would be honored by the goldsmiths of Venice. This was the beginning of banking.

Sometimes a special employee would sit outside of the goldsmiths' shop, or in the marketplace, accepting and returning deposits. The benches where they sat were called bancos, the word which became our modern word, bank.

*A representation of an early mint*
*in Northern Europe, around 1500*

# 4     *History of U.S. Mint and Coins*

Most early settlers in North America bartered with furs, shells or iron nails, but as soon as cities began forming as a result of increased trade, there was a demand for coins. The first coins minted in America were made during the 1600s. Many of these coins were in circulation even before George Washington was born. But "homemade" coins were generally very scarce and many people used foreign coins.

Even though the United States were then colonies of England, the Spanish "dollar," the *real*, was the most popular coin. This was probably because it had a higher content of pure silver than any other European coin. Like Athens, thousands of years earlier, Spain had control of the richest silver mines in the world. It was the first European country to coin money in the New World, setting up mints in Mexico and Peru. The early American coin makers copied the real when they made the first American dollars. And in some ways, our modern money system is still based on the real, nicknamed "pieces of eight." It was easily broken into quarters or two bits which is how our American quarter got its nickname.

Early American coins were rarely taken at face value because parts of them were often clipped off and so they didn't have their full weight. Because the early American coins weren't trusted, foreign coins stayed in circulation for a long time.

The first state-operated mint established in America was started in Boston (in the mid-1600s) by order of the Massachusetts Bay Court. It did not have the approval of the king of England and was considered a very daring move at the time. The coins made at this mint were in English denominations (amounts), of a shilling (12 pence or pennies), six pence, and three pence. Compared with the beautifully made coins of Europe, these small tokens were crude, and worse yet, were easily counterfeited. Coins of the same value from the same mint often did not look the same because they were so badly made. The coins were made in the same way as ancient coins. Circles of metal (blanks) were placed into a die (or pattern) and struck with a hammer. The only design on them was a number that showed how much the coin was worth, and the initials N.E. for New England; and only the shilling piece was marked with the number. Something had to be done to make American coins more popular so the people running the mint decided to decorate each coin with the design of a tree, either a willow, oak or pine tree. These coins were in circulation for about 30 years in and around Boston, but they always were minted with the date of the first year they were made, 1652. Each state continued to make its own coins until the first U.S. mint started its operations in Philadelphia, over a hundred years later.

The Mint Act of April 1792 called for gold coins to be made in amounts of $10, $5, and $2.50; silver coins of $1, 50¢, 25¢, 10¢ and 5¢; and copper coins of 1¢ and ½¢. A staff was hired and it took only a year for the mint to set up and begin production. But it was making only copper coins: one-cent and half-cent pieces. This is because neither the coiner, Henry Voigt, who made the coins or the assayer, Albion Cox, who examined the quality of the metals used, could post a $10,000 bond which was needed before they could use gold or silver in their work. This $10,000 bond was needed by the U.S. government to ensure that neither Cox or Voigt would secretly steal raw precious metals or mint less-than-full weight coins. After another year had passed and they still couldn't post the bond, the directors of the mint lowered the amount to $1000, and minting got underway. But even so, during 1794 only a few thousand silver coins were minted. Legend has it that President George Washington gave his own silverware to make the first coins, five-cent pieces called half-dismes. It was many years though until the mint was producing a full range of coins.

David Rittenhouse was the first director of the mint; he was born in Pennsylvania and was a watchmaker, astronomer, mathematician, and engraver. The first mint equipment was imported from England and required horses to supply the power required to operate the machines! Some federal budget items from that period include horse medicine and straw.

The mint workers put in long hours, often from sunup to sundown, for the natural light. In the evening, light was provided by candles, lamps, and fireplaces. And during the winter months, many mint workers stayed at their places day and night tending the equipment so that it wouldn't freeze.

To stop thefts from the mint, once workers arrived there at, say, 6 A.M., they weren't allowed to leave for any reason until their shift was over, usually around 7 or 8 P.M. And guards would search all workers going in or out of the mint. If they left their dinner at home, it had to stay there unless a friend or relative could bring it around to them.

The first step to automation came in 1836 when coins were steam pressed for the first time. The mint's production of U.S. coins was not able to keep up with the demand. Many of the larger denomination coins (half-dollar pieces and more) of gold and silver were treated as if they were bullion (precious metal bricks) and were held on to, circulated as bank reserves, or exchanged for worn or clipped foreign coins and shipped out of the country for

*David Rittenhouse, first director of the U.S. Mint*

reminting. There may have been less than one coin, of any amount, per person in 1830.

The money circulating in America from about 1794 to 1834 included foreign gold and silver coins, many of which were worth less than their face value, bank notes from individual banks, and small federal silver coins. In 1834 a law was passed setting a standard weight for gold coins. This allowed branch mints to be opened in North Carolina and Georgia near newly opened gold mines. This helped end the coin shortage by enabling more coins to be produced in more locations, instead of just one; the gold produced at these mines could be minted into coins much sooner since it didn't have to be shipped across the country.

Gold was discovered in California in 1848 and soon another branch mint was opened there to mint gold coming in from the mines in the western states. The many gold and silver coins produced by the 1850s were finally enough to meet the needs of commerce.

The Civil War changed all that, though. Because of the war, people began saving coins, or any hard currency. There was so little money in circulation that communities began using postage stamps as small change. The warning you sometimes see, asking you to not send postage stamps for mail-order purchases, dates back to this period. Also, during this time, some stores issued their own money or trade tokens. The federal government tried to ease this new money crisis by printing paper "greenbacks" in the same denominations (amounts) as the coins. However, these bills were not redeemable in gold or silver; this increased the value of the metals even more, and a silver dollar often bought $1.25 worth of goods—or even more.

As little money as there was circulating in the North during the Civil War, there was much less in the South. The Confederacy had almost no money in their treasury. Even though early in the war it had seized the U.S. Mint in New Orleans, along with its bullion, the precious metals only made up a small part of the billions of dollars of paper currency that was issued by the Confederacy. As a result, there was very little of the precious metal to back its currency. They had hoped to earn more gold and silver by exporting cotton to Europe, but the Northern blockade of their ports prevented that. As the bales of unshipped cotton piled up in warehouses, the value of Confederate money dropped. Confederate problems were made worse by counterfeiters who sometimes offered as much as $2,000 in Southern currency for 50¢ . . . which was 50¢ more than it was worth.

After the war was over, during the Reconstruction period, demand was still high for coins made of precious metal. And paper currency, once thought of as temporary emergency money, was still issued by the federal government. Finally in 1878, enough new silver dollars were minted in the Morgan series (named after the artist who created the coin's portrait of Liberty) to meet public demand.

*A twenty dollar note, issued by the Confederate States of America. The note promises to pay the bearer "six months after the ratification of a treaty of peace," a promise that could not be kept by the defeated Confederacy.*

## COINS ISSUED TODAY
## BY THE
## UNITED STATES MINT

| Coin | Value | Face | Reverse |
|---|---|---|---|
| Penny | One cent | Abraham Lincoln | Lincoln Memorial |
| Nickel | Five cents | Thomas Jefferson | Monticello |
| Dime | Ten cents | Franklin Delano Roosevelt | Torch and olive branch |
| Quarter | Twenty-five cents | George Washington | American Eagle |
| Half-dollar | Fifty cents | John F. Kennedy | Great Seal of the United States |
| Dollar | One hundred cents | no one-dollar coins are currently being minted | |

Except during the Civil War, there were few changes made in the coins issued by the U.S. mints. The first big change in the history of our coins came when a portrait of Lincoln was reproduced on the copper one-cent piece in 1909. This was the first picture of a real person, living or dead, that had ever appeared on a U.S. coin. As a matter of fact, it's against the law to place the portrait of a living person on a U.S. coin or bill. Within a short period of time, the nickel, dime and quarter were all redesigned. By 1955, Congress passed a law that the motto "In God We Trust" (which first appeared on a two-cent piece in 1864) must appear on all U.S. coins.

In 1965 another big change in U.S. coins was made when dimes and quarters—once made mostly of silver—were changed to copper, with a nickel and copper outer shell. More recently, in celebration of the American Bicentennial in 1976, 25¢ and 50¢ pieces were minted with two dates: 1776 and 1976. In 1979 the Susan B. Anthony dollar was introduced. This dollar has the first portrait of a famous woman on a coin (there was a very early Martha Washington $1 bill issued in the 1880s). As of now, the Anthony dollar is very unpopular because it is very easy to confuse it with a less-valuable quarter. They're both the same color and just about the same size and shape. The Anthony dollar may be discontinued. In 1983 the U.S. Mint began issuing copper-clad zinc pennies. These pennies look the same as older pennies, but no longer have a high copper content.

Today, the U.S. mints are located in Philadelphia, Denver, and San Francisco. Our mints have machines that can make up to 10,000 pennies per minute and are the fastest in the world. The U.S. mints also make coins for Canada, Israel, El Salvador, and Liberia.

No matter what inflation does to the value of a U.S. dollar there are still the same amount of coins in it: one hundred pennies, twenty nickels, ten dimes, four quarters, two half-dollars, and one dollar coin all make up one dollar.

# 5 History of Paper Money and U.S. Paper Money

Most, but not all, monies issued throughout history have been coins, although they, of course, have been the most long-lasting form of currency. Money has been printed on clay tablets, silk, leather, and paper. Some of the earliest "paper" (non-coin) money was issued in China around the middle of the thirteenth century. In fact, the famous Italian explorer, Marco Polo, reported that a Chinese emperor, Kublai Khan, had issued paper money that had his personal red seal and the signature of his treasurer. The notes were as valuable as silver or gold coins and could be exchanged for new notes when they became worn or dirty. This and later money contained a warning that counterfeiting was punishable by death and offered a reward to anyone who turned in a counterfeiter.

"Paper" money is a kind of money whose writing is more valuable than what it is being written on; so, in a way, coins became the first "paper" money when the inscription on them became more important than their actual precious metal value. Today there are three ingredients that make up paper money: engravings, ink, and paper. Ink has been around for over 4,000 years. Lampblack was mixed with glue to make a crude form of ink in ancient Egypt, even before papyrus was used. The combination of papyrus and lampblack wasn't any good for money. Papyrus was a kind of paper made from a water weed, was very brittle, and too fragile to stand up to repeated use; lampblack was not permanent ink and it smudged. The Chinese invented real paper, as we know it, around 100 A.D. They used the paper for money which was handwritten. The process of engraving had to be invented before paper money could become really popular.

An engraving is made by cutting fine lines into metal plates, which are then covered with ink. When the ink is wiped off the face of the plate, some remains in the fine lines. That ink will transfer to a piece of paper pressed on the plate. Paper money often has very fancy and complicated designs and many pieces of money—all exactly alike—can be made from the same engraving plate. A really fine engraving containing many swirling lines lessens the chance of counterfeiting the bills because it is really hard to exactly copy a good engraving.

While the use of engravings does make the *best* kind of paper money, some kinds of paper money have been around almost as long as the written word. For example, IOUs are a kind of money, but real money is issued to the general public rather than to one person, either by a bank or a government. Sweden issued the first European bank note in the seventeenth century, but it wasn't very popular. It was a good invention, but it took a long time to really catch on.

Even though the U.S. government didn't begin to issue paper money until 1861, paper money of one kind or another has always been in circulation here. Many kinds of notes issued while we were still under English rule could be redeemed in foreign coins. After the Declaration of Independence, the Continental Congress issued Continental currency. Most people did not believe that the new government could back its paper money with gold or silver and so it was not very popular and not worth very much either!

For many decades after the revolutionary war, the U.S. government issued only coins. During this period, from about 1790 to 1860, many state banks issued paper money on their own, in the form of bank notes. These notes were used locally to pay for ser-

The paper money issued by the
Continental Congress was
generally considered worthless
and gave rise to the expression,
"Not worth a continental."

vices or merchandise just like paper currency is used today. This wasn't the best paper currency system though, because the farther away you were from the bank that issued the money, the less the bank note was worth. And because of bad investments, big debts, and other problems, these banks could and did go broke; this left the bank notes with no value at all, since there was then no bank backing it.

All paper money and savings bonds are printed today by the United States Bureau of Engraving and Printing. The bureau also prints postage stamps, invitations to White House parties, Coast Guard diplomas, and other official government documents. The bureau was started in 1861 when the federal government began printing paper money again to replace the coins then being hoarded. This federal money was popular because coins were very scarce and most people trusted the federal government bills more than those issued by local banks. So the government just never stopped printing it. Soon many banks which had been printing bank notes stopped issuing them.

All U.S. money is printed on special paper made of 75 percent cotton and 25 percent linen. The paper also has many small red and blue threads pressed into it to make counterfeiting more difficult. It takes several engravers, who have all studied for years, to complete one plate or die which makes up a printing master roll. The bills are printed on a high-speed press which can hold as many as 10,000 blank sheets of paper at one time. Thirty-two bills are printed on one sheet. One side of the bill is printed with green ink and the next day black ink is printed on the other side. Ink that is used by the United States in printing money is made from a secret formula. When the printing is finished, each bill is inspected by hand; any imperfect bills are removed and destroyed. From start to finish, each bill is checked for defects numerous times. When a bill is destroyed the serial number is still used, but the new bill's number is printed with a star in front of it to show that it is a replacement bill.

*Secretary of the Treasury Donald Regan and U.S. Treasurer
Katherine Ortega inspect a sheet of one dollar bills,
fresh off the press at the Bureau of Engraving.*

## U.S BILLS
## PRINTED TODAY

| Amount | Face | Back |
|---|---|---|
| $1 | George Washington | Great Seal |
| $2 | Thomas Jefferson | Signing of the Declaration of Independence |
| $5 | Abraham Lincoln | Lincoln Memorial |
| $10 | Alexander Hamilton | U.S Treasury Building |
| $20 | Andrew Jackson | White House |
| $50 | Ulysses S. Grant | U.S. Capitol Building |
| $100 | Benjamin Franklin | Independence Hall |
| $500 | William McKinley | Amount of Bill |
| $1,000 | Grover Cleveland | Amount of Bill |
| $5,000 | James Madison | Amount of Bill |
| $10,000 | Salmon P. Chase | Amount of Bill |
| $100,000 | Woodrow Wilson | Amount of Bill |

Here are some interesting facts about our paper money. About one-half of all the bills printed are in the $1 denomination, and each bill is expected to last for twenty-two months. Each year the Bureau of Engraving and Printing uses almost 5,000 tons of paper and 2,000 tons of ink while making paper money. That's 14 million pounds of money every year.

The printed colors of U.S. money are black and green. The faces of all the bills are standard, each containing a portrait of a great American. Except for the $1 bill which carries the great seal on the reverse and the $2 bill which has a picture of the signing of the Declaration of Independence, all bills of $100 or less have pictures of important U.S. buildings such as the White House, Capitol, and Lincoln Memorial, on the reverse. As a matter of fact, if you look very carefully at the engraving of the Lincoln Memorial, on the $5 bill, you can find the names of the forty-eight mainland states on the top-front of the building. Bills of larger amounts all have their dollar amounts on the reverse, but these bills are somewhat rare and are not in general circulation. The size of the modern U.S. bills are 6⅛″ by 2⅝″.

When money is worn out or damaged, it is sent to the U.S. Federal Reserve Banks to be shredded and burned. If three-fifths or more of a damaged bill remains, the government will replace it with a new one. If less than that amount, but more than two-fifths of the bill remains, you can get a 50 percent refund.

Strangely enough, around the turn of this century, the mint washed, ironed, and reissued dirty paper money instead of destroying it!

The letters which appear in the Federal Reserve seal in the middle of the left hand side of the face of all U.S. bills and the letter leading the bill's serial number must agree. This letter is a Federal Reserve code letter and it shows where the bill was circulated. It's interesting to check and see how far a bill has traveled. Here's a list of the Federal Reserve code letters and the places they stand for:

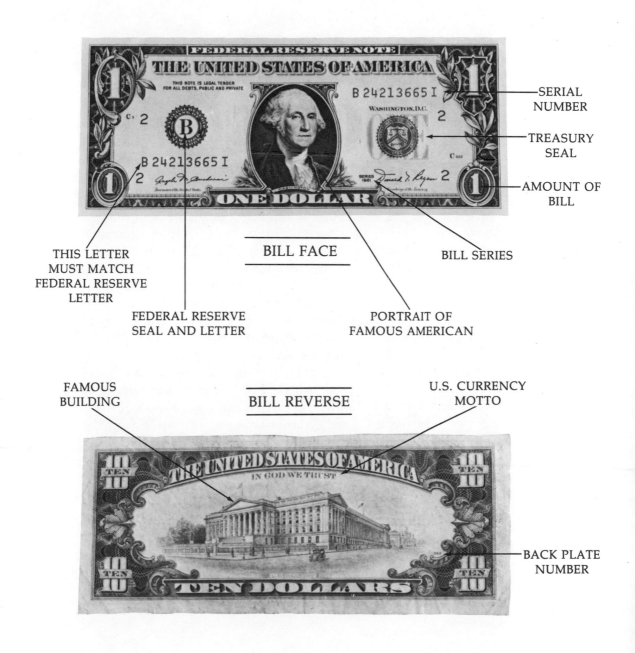

SERIAL NUMBER

TREASURY SEAL

AMOUNT OF BILL

BILL SERIES

BILL FACE

THIS LETTER MUST MATCH FEDERAL RESERVE LETTER

FEDERAL RESERVE SEAL AND LETTER

PORTRAIT OF FAMOUS AMERICAN

FAMOUS BUILDING

U.S. CURRENCY MOTTO

BILL REVERSE

BACK PLATE NUMBER

| A | Boston | G | Chicago |
|---|--------|---|---------|
| B | New York | H | St. Louis |
| C | Philadelphia | I | Minneapolis |
| D | Cleveland | J | Kansas City |
| E | Richmond | K | Dallas |
| F | Atlanta | L | San Francisco |

The $1 bill reverse side contains both the front and the back of the Great Seal of the United States, which was designed and adopted over two hundred years ago.

The front of the seal is on the right side of the back of the bill. It shows our national bird, the bald eagle, holding an olive branch in its right talon and arrows in its left talon. The olive branch contains thirteen leaves and thirteen berries and there are thirteen arrows. This number stands for the number of original American colonies. A ribbon in the eagle's mouth contains the motto "E Pluribus Unum" which means "One out of many." This refers to the one country formed from the thirteen colonies. Over the bird's head are thirteen, five-pointed stars surrounded by clouds.

The reverse of the seal appears on the left side of the back of the $1 bill. The roman number MDCCLXXVI is on the bottom of the pyramid; this is 1776, the year when the Declaration of Independence was signed. The pyramid was left unfinished on the seal to show that the country would still be growing. The eye in the very top of the pyramid stands for an all-seeing God, which would be watching over our country to protect it, and the motto above the eye, "Annuit Coeptis," means "God has favored our undertakings." The motto on the bottom of the pyramid, "Novus Ordo Seclorum," means "A new order of the ages," which refers to the new United States of America starting a new kind of government by the people.

# 6

## What Are Banks?

The places most people think of, when they think of money, are banks. Banks handle most people's money business such as making car and home loans, issuing bank charge cards, supplying safe deposit boxes for storing valuables, and furnishing checking and savings accounts. Banks are the safest and best place to keep your money.

Banks want people to store their money there, so they pay interest on the money. That is, if you put $100 in the bank at 5 percent interest per year, the bank will pay you $105 at the end of that time.

How can the bank afford to do this? By lending your $100 to another bank customer who is willing to pay the bank 12 percent, say, to borrow that $100. After a year, that customer must pay the bank $112, the loan plus the interest. After subtracting the $5 paid out to you in interest the bank earns a $7 profit.

Many, many people deposit hundreds of thousands of dollars a year in banks and others borrow just as much. This is how banks make their profit. Some of this profit goes to paying rent on the bank building, some to the salaries of bank workers, and some is kept in reserve to help insure loans. But a bank's main job is to store cash and pay it out easily.

There are four main kinds of banks:

## COMMERCIAL BANKS

These banks offer many different kinds of services: checking, savings accounts, loans, credit cards, and more. They're called commercial banks because they originally only had business customers. Today, however, they have private customers, too. Any kind of banking service you can think of can be found today at a commercial bank, which is the oldest kind of bank in America.

## SAVINGS BANKS

These banks were started almost 200 years ago to offer savings accounts to the people who did not bank at commercial banks. Many savings banks have the words dollar or dime in their name. Or they may have the name of the kind of customer, a seaman or merchant or emigrant, for example, who they hoped would bank with them. These banks were willing to accept small deposits. They are mostly found in the northeastern states and have charters in seventeen states. Today they offer many of the same kinds of services and accounts as commercial banks.

## SAVINGS AND LOANS

This kind of bank started about 150 years ago. They are mostly in the business of making home mortgage loans. They make more mortgage loans each year than the other types of banks combined. This kind of bank was started by people who put their money together. Their idea was for all of them to take turns borrowing the money to build their homes. Because of this, they were once called building and loan banks.

*This boy is making a deposit at the convenient drive-in window of his bank.*

# CREDIT UNIONS

This type of bank has been very popular in the last forty or fifty years. Credit unions may pay higher interest on savings accounts and may charge less for loans. A credit union is usually started by a group of people who have something in common, such as living in the same town or working for the same company. Most members of credit unions know one another and this lessens the chances of unpaid loans, perhaps because loan takers may feel more responsible toward neighbors and co-workers and would be less likely to default on a loan from them, rather than one from an impersonal bank.

# 7 *History of U.S. Banks*

American banks have always needed a charter . . . or license to operate. Every state can issue a charter to a bank wanting to start up within that state. The charter will show how much money the bank needed to begin operating and what the bank might and might not do with the deposits.

It wasn't always easy to get a charter from a state government to open a bank. Years ago, a bank was thought of as a business that printed paper money—and paper money wasn't trusted. Two hundred years ago many politicians hoped that the United States would allow only metal coins to be used, so that all the banks would go out of business.

At different times in U.S. history, some states had no banks at all, or no laws to govern private banks, or banks with state charters which allowed them to print money.

One of the biggest costs of starting up a bank in the mid-1800s was paper and ink for bank notes. As a matter of fact, there were companies which sold designs for paper money, or bank notes, much the same way that wallpaper is sold today—designs were chosen from a sample book. The American Bank Note Company was one of the largest and most popular money engravers. They offered engravings of flowers, leaves, popular celebrities of the day, and patriots, as well as scenes from great battles or everyday life. Colors of the money varied from red to blue to green, as well as other in-between colors. Banks used their own notes for everything from employee salaries to rent for their offices.

The first "modern" bank in the United States opened in Philadelphia in 1782. It was the Bank of North America, chartered in the state of Pennsylvania. The charter said that it should have $10,000,000 in assets but it began operating with only $400,000, of which more than half came from the government. This was an important bank, not only because it printed currency, but because it helped to finance the last part of the American Revolution. Within ten years after the Bank of North America opened there were fourteen banks in the United States, each having assets of about $1,000,000.

In 1791, the new federal government chartered and operated the first Bank of the United States which operated successfully until 1811. Its main office was in Philadelphia and it had branches in leading cities in the thirteen new states. It was responsible for financing many of the new businesses springing up in our new land. The Bank of the United States closed after twenty years because the government could not decide whether it wanted to be in the banking business or not, so it just allowed the charter to expire. But the closing of the Bank of the United States did not affect state banks. Between 1811 and 1863 as our country grew, the number of state banks grew, too.

The National Banking Act of 1863, however, allowed the federal government to begin issuing bank charters again. This time the requirements were that any group of five or more could start a bank if they had $50,000 to $250,000, depending on the size of the city where they wanted to start the bank. These were "national" banks and had to use that word in their name. They also had to follow many rules for managing their money that the state banks were not required to do in their charters.

Once this system was in place, private banks stopped issuing paper money because the National Banking Act also called for a

10 percent tax on any bank that cashed private bank notes. This made the private money business unprofitable.

From 1864 to 1866 the number of federal banks grew from 139 to 1,582 and the number of state banks dropped from 1,089 to 297.

An interesting fact is that Secretary of the Treasury Salmon P. Chase, in Lincoln's administration, was the person who wrote the National Banking Act. He is thought to be the father of today's banking system in the United States. His portrait appears on the $10,000 bill, one of the only portraits of a person who was neither a president or an early American patriot. As a matter of fact, the huge Chase Manhattan Bank headquartered in New York was named after him, too.

Banks, in general, found that it was more profitable to lend out the money they held on deposit for interest, than to make a profit by issuing bank notes. And as many people began to put their trust—and their money—in banks, they grew in size, influence, and wealth.

As the western frontier was settled by the pioneers, without a doubt one of the first businesses to open would be a bank. So while the country was growing, so did the number of banks. Communication was slow a hundred years ago and many banks charged high fees for cashing out-of-town checks; or the banks wouldn't cash them at all because it took too long for them to get their money—if they ever got it at all—from the bank the check was drawn on.

In the years before the turn of the century, there were several panics and depressions caused by the lack of communication between banks. For example, if several large depositors in Ohio wanted to withdraw all their money in cash to make a purchase, the bank could not give the money back, if much of the bank reserves were tied up in out-of-state checks which had already been paid out, but had not yet cleared. In the days before the Federal Reserve System it could take several weeks for a check to

*Miners bring in gold dust to be weighed
at a frontier bank in Denver, Colorado.*

return to its home bank and for the money to reach the bank where it was cashed. This might cause a rumor that the bank had no money. Many depositors would rush to the bank demanding to withdraw their money. When the bank ran out of hard cash, they would simply have to close for good.

In 1910, a commission was set up to study this problem. It recommended that the United States start a central bank, much like those in Europe and other parts of the world. The U.S. central bank is the Federal Reserve Bank, sometimes called "the Fed." The Federal Reserve System is still very much in existence today, but you can't open an account at the Federal Reserve Bank.

# 8 The U.S. Federal Reserve System

The Federal Reserve System divides the country into twelve districts. Each bank that is a customer of the system sends its money to the central bank for its district. This central bank acts as a clearinghouse (that is, it sorts out all the checks and sends them back to the bank they were drawn on). It cashes the checks and transfers the money from one bank to another in that district. The Federal Reserve Banks are sometimes known as "banker's banks" because they provide service to the banking community not the general public.

A commercial bank can borrow extra money from the Fed to lend to a customer. The Fed charges the bank the lowest interest rate that it can. This is called the discount rate, or the best rate they have. The commercial bank must then charge more than the discount rate to make a profit. When the discount rate is high, as it was in the early 1980s, it is very expensive to borrow money from the Federal Reserve System. This stops or discourages people from borrowing and we say that money is "tight."

Bank loans are an important asset in helping the nation's economy to grow. They allow people to make large purchases which keep factories in business. These businesses pay their employees, who then spend money. The circulation of money in this way is what keeps our economy healthy.

If money in the economy is too available, there is inflation and prices of goods in stores can increase rapidly because there is more money than goods. If there is not very much money in circulation, people cannot spend cash and then there is a recession, and the same goods may drop in price. The Federal Reserve System controls the money supply in the United States and if the economy is working right, store prices should not change very much from year to year. When prices are stable so is our money.

Another organization set up by the federal government to protect our money is the FDIC, which stands for the Federal Deposit Insurance Corporation. In 1933, during the Great Depression in this country, which was a gigantic recession, many people could not pay banks back for their loans. This meant that those banks didn't have enough cash to give to people who wanted to withdraw their deposits. Because of this, many banks were forced to close and it looked as if many more banks in the United States might go out of business. In fact, thousands of banks did close permanently and many depositors lost their life savings.

To make sure that this terrible situation would never happen again, the government started the FDIC, which today insures each account in a commercial bank up to a limit of $100,000. Savings and Loans banks also have insurance called SLDIC (Savings and Loans Deposit Insurance Corporation) which also protects deposits up to the same amount.

The FDIC and SLDIC insure losses caused by fire or theft as well as bank closings. Ninety-eight percent of all the banks in the United States carry some kind of insurance.

The Federal Reserve System performs several other important functions, too. It clears checks for its bank customers, and holds excess money for them in safekeeping. The U.S. government deposits its tax money and the Fed supplies the government with regional banks for its checks so that they do not all have to come from Washington, D.C. It supervises local banks, audits their

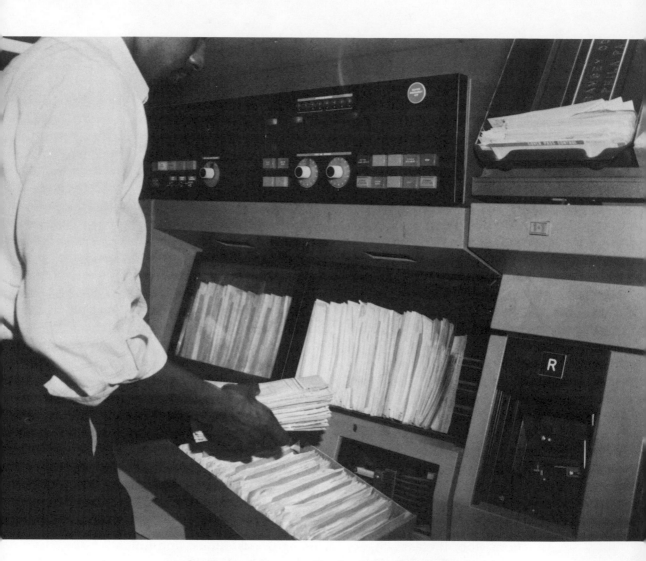

At the Federal Reserve Bank of New York, checks are
sent through a high-speed machine which sorts them
according to a number printed in magnetic ink at
the bottom of each check. The number indicates
the bank upon which the check is drawn.

books, and makes sure that member banks are following the banking laws. It does financial research and gives out information about the economy to member banks, government officials, educators, and private citizens. The Fed also carries out the government's money policies.

At the time the Fed was established, all banks chartered by the federal government (the banks with the word "national" in their name) were required to join. Many state banks joined, too. But many did not because one of the requirements of joining the Fed was placing a large low-interest-bearing reserve on deposit in the district's bank. If interest rates are high, a bank stands to lose a lot of money this way. The Fed deposits these funds in interest-bearing accounts and earns about seven billion dollars a year on these deposits, an important source of money to the U.S. Treasury.

# 9

## The History
## of Checking

No one is really sure, but checking may have started with the ancient Romans. Most banking history experts agree though, that checks, as we know them today, first became popular during the seventeenth century. Wealthy merchants who left their gold with goldsmiths, received notes from the goldsmith. A customer could, and did, send notes to the goldsmith asking him, for example, to pay 100 pieces of gold to another person.

This was the start of checking.

An early problem with this system was that merchants had to go from goldsmith to goldsmith to collect the money from the notes. This problem was solved by hiring messengers to make the collections. Each day a messenger made many trips, and also got to know messengers from other goldsmiths, merchants and banks. It's only natural that someone had the idea to meet in a central location to exchange checks. This was the first bank clearinghouse and clearinghouses today operate in much the same way. Each bank in the clearinghouse's district sends clerks to deliver other banks' checks and to pay the amount they owe or collect the money they are owed. Once, the settlements were made in cash, but today funds are transferred electronically by computer.

The United States uses more checks than any other country in the world. Checking in the United States began while our nation was still a colony of England, but it didn't become a widespread way of business until after the Revolution. By the mid-nineteenth century there were more checks in use than paper money or coins. But because there was no central clearinghouse, there were problems sometimes between banks exchanging checks. Some banks wanted to charge a service fee for processing out-of-town checks. Other banks took a very long time to process their checks.

The creation of the Federal Reserve System in 1913 did help to make check writing easier and quicker, but even today, it may be a problem to cash a California check in Rhode Island, or a Texas check in Wisconsin. More and more consumers are using electronic banking systems or credit cards to avoid this problem.

Still most people today use checking accounts when spending their money. Checks are as easy to use and as widely accepted for purchases as paper money or coins. Most people just take them for granted. Although most people write their checks on a standard form, anything with the proper information entered on it, such as to whom it is payable, the date, amount of the check, name and address of your bank and your account number, and your signature, can be used as a check. There are stories about people who have made out checks on giant stones, or on their clothes, and these kinds of checks were negotiable.

A check should always be made out in ink so that the specified dollar amount cannot be changed. When a check is written out, the dollar amount should be spelled out on the middle line and written in numbers in the upper-right-hand side. Your name, address and (sometimes) your telephone number are usually printed on the check in the upper-left-hand corner. On the upper right-hand corner is the check number and right below that is a space for the date. On the bottom right-hand corner is a space for your signature. When you are making out a check, make sure to fill in all the blank lines with the proper information.

A check is "endorsed" when the person who is being paid signs the back of the check.

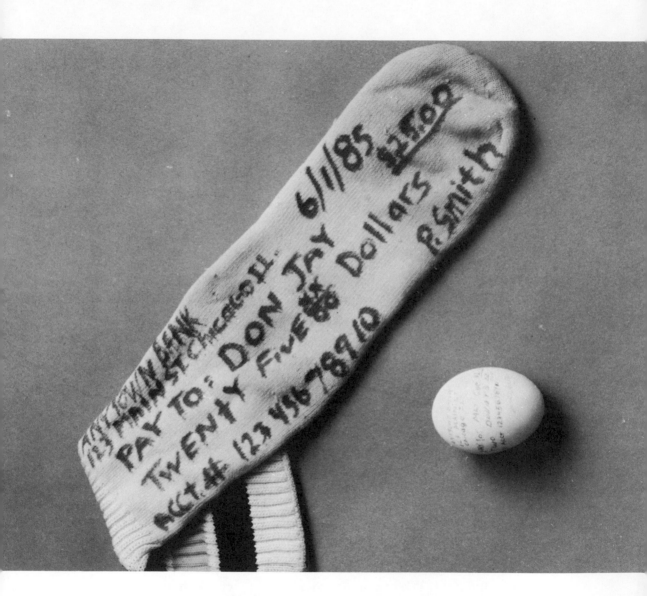

*Checks may be written on anything,*
*as long as the information is correct.*

If you don't have any (or enough) money in your checking account, when a check is returned to your bank for collection it will "bounce" instead. That means it will go back to the person it was written out to without payment.

If you change your mind about paying someone after you have sent a check, you can "stop payment" on it, then it cannot be cashed.

You can "certify" a check to make sure it is good. This is done by a bank stamping a check showing that there is money in the account which they will put aside to cover the check's amount.

Today, Americans write about 34 billion checks a year. That's thirty trillion checkbook dollars in circulation in the United States or 135 million checks written every business day.

One way that the process of sorting checks is speeded up is the row of computer numbers printed on the bottom of every printed check. The first two numbers in the row show the bank's Federal Reserve district, the third number stands for the Federal Reserve branch bank, and the fourth shows what state the check is from. The next four numbers are the bank's code identification number. The ninth number is one which must agree with other numbers in the row to show that the check is not counterfeit. The next nine numbers show your checking account number and the four after that are the check number. The final numbers are the dollar amount of the check. These numbers are printed onto the check by the first bank that receives it. The printed numbers on the upper right-hand corner of the check are used for sorting by hand. The numbers on the bottom of the check make it possible for a machine to sort as many as 100,000 checks an hour.

But even so, today the Federal Reserve Bank in New York City hires workers around the clock, to process eight million checks every day. That's about seven billion dollars or fourteen tons of checkbook money. There are forty-six regional Federal Reserve check-processing locations, so you can get an idea of the huge number of checks being processed every day.

*This man is using a bank card to withdraw
money from an Automatic Teller Machine.*

By 1990, the number of checks circulating every year is expected to reach forty billion! Without electronic banking there would probably be more paper checks circulating than it would be possible to process.

Today, banking customers can use Automatic Teller Machines, or ATMs, twenty-four hours a day to transfer money, make a deposit or withdrawal, or to just check their account balance. This is just the beginning of electronic banking in our society. Stores are beginning to offer a cashless and checkless payment process, with a debit card which makes an automatic transfer of money from a customer's bank account to the store's bank account. It is very possible that by the turn of the century, checks will almost be replaced by electronic money transfers.

Not only are consumers glad to use checks, but checking account money helps to increase the money supply in the country as well. When you deposit cash in a checking account, the bank does not set your money aside in a vault separate from all their other accounts. Instead, they enter the amount you're depositing in their records and place your account money into their general funds. The bank holds back a certain amount as a reserve and they use the rest as loans to businesses and individuals. So, for example, if you deposit $1,000 in your checking account at the "Littlecity" bank, the bank may hold back 10 percent or $100 in reserve and lend the other $900 to another customer who may want help to pay for her vacation. That customer (after depositing the money in her account) can then write a $900 check to an airline company for tickets to Hawaii. The airline company deposits the $900 in their account in the "Bigcity" bank. The "Bigcity" bank now has another $900 in their general funds. If they hold back 10 percent or $90 in reserve, the bank can now lend out $810 to another customer. In this way, the money supply grows without any extra currency being coined or printed. Most U.S. money is checkbook money. It appears on paper records, but does not really exist.

# 10 All About Credit Cards

Another kind of payment system in the United States today, other than barter, cash or checks is the use of plastic credit cards. The first bank credit card was issued in California in 1959, making it the newest kind of money. And since that time they have become so popular that there may now be as many as 780 million credit cards in use today. That's about three cards for every man, woman and child in this country. On the average, each of these people makes over 1,000 cash, 250 check, and fifty credit card purchases each year.

A bank credit card, like MasterCard or Visa is an agreement with a bank which allows you to buy goods and services with the bank's money. You then have the choice of paying the loan back right away or continuing to borrow the money at an agreed rate of interest, which usually is the highest allowed by law, sometimes as high as 20 percent per year or more!

The use of credit cards is a popular and very easy way to pay for the things you buy. It is a system that is good for everyone involved. A small merchant might make a credit card sale that he wouldn't have made if the purchase had to be made in cash. The bank will probably earn interest on the loan and the purchaser will be able to stretch his budget. Bank credit cards are accepted in many places for food, travel, clothing and entertainment. These

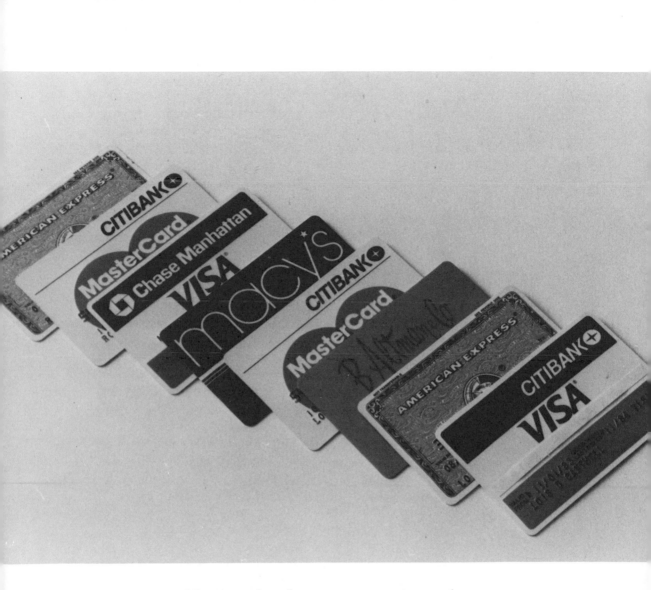

*Many people today carry an assortment of
credit cards that allow them to make
purchases without using cash or checks—
at least until the monthly bill arrives!*

cards offer a "credit limit" or a fixed maximum amount that you can charge.

About half of the credit cards in use today are for private store charges, such as those offered by Sears or Macy's. The bank cards, MasterCard and Visa, account for another 100 million cards. The rest are oil company, auto, airline, travel and entertainment cards. The bank cards are all standard pieces of plastic, all the same size and shape. A Visa card issued in Maine will be exactly the same size and shape as a MasterCard issued in Nevada. But each kind of card may be a different size, shape, thickness and color.

Debit cards are also becoming popular. This kind of card allows the user to charge a purchase to his bank account rather than borrow, and pay interest on money for small purchases. A debit card is used exactly like a charge card, but *acts* like a check. A consumer would receive a receipt at the time of purchase and an itemized statement at the end of the month. But no paper would circulate from buyer to merchant to bank to Fed, back to the bank and back to the buyer. And the consumer would not receive a bundle of canceled checks at the end of the month. It is this system people have in mind when they predict that electronic banking will someday replace checks.

The debit card would also provide a handy identification card for people who do not have charge cards or driver's licenses. Many people think that the special bank cards used today for Automatic Teller Machines will someday become debit cards.

# 11 The Counterfeiting Problem

Counterfeiting is a problem that has been around for a long time. As long as there has been money, there has been someone trying to copy it. This is because there are great profits to be made in fake money. If someone in ancient Rome, say, could make a fake gold coin out of another less-valuable metal and use it like a real coin, he would wind up with a profit. Even some rulers have been counterfeiters. The Roman emperor, Nero, may have been one of the greatest counterfeiters of all time. He produced coins which looked real, but that contained much less precious metal. The extra gold, missing from the coins, went into Nero's pocket. Even some of our early settlers were counterfeiters, making fake wampum to trade with the local Indians. At one time there was a factory in New Jersey that made strings of counterfeit shells.

While not strictly counterfeiting, coin clipping was a problem which had been around for centuries also, lessening the value of money. Clipped coins have had small pieces of silver or gold shaved from their edges. As one person after another does this to a coin, it becomes smaller and smaller as it circulates. Even coin makers were thought to clip coins before sending them out into circulation.

A famous economist of the sixteenth century, Sir Thomas Gresham, had a theory about the effects of coin clipping on the money of a nation. The theory, or Gresham's law, is that "Bad money will drive out good." As clipping became more widespread, some people began weighing coins and removing the heaviest ones from circulation. So the "bad" or clipped coins, drove the "good" or full-weight coins out of general circulation because people saved them, instead of spending them. After all, if one silver coin weighs one ounce, as it is supposed to, and another coin with the same value only weighs 7/8 of an ounce, the coin with the full weight is really worth more. Many people who saved the heavier-weight coins melted them down and made gold bricks or ingots from them.

And at one point in English history, the clipping problem got to be so bad that the king ordered that all coin makers who could not prove that they had *not* been clipping coins would have their right hands cut off. That action solved the problem, at least for the time.

Clipping is rarely, if ever, done to U.S. coins today, because our coins are no longer made of precious metals. But the practice was stopped long before that, when most of our coins began having reeded edges. Reeding is a series of fine lines, perpendicular to the coins surface, which covers the entire edge of the coins.

Counterfeiting coins is another practice that has all but died out in modern times. The main reason for this is that it may be more expensive to make fake coins than it is to buy real ones. But once in a while a dishonest person will make counterfeit collectors' coins, copies of an old or rare coin that would be worth many times the value of the raw material used. Most fake coins are not as sharply detailed as real ones.

Paper bills are a different story, though. Paper and ink are not expensive and profits on fake bills can be huge. During the Civil War, as much as one-third of all the paper money in circulation was counterfeit. The U.S. Secret Service was formed in 1865 to help fight this problem and continues to fight counterfeiting today. They also protect our president.

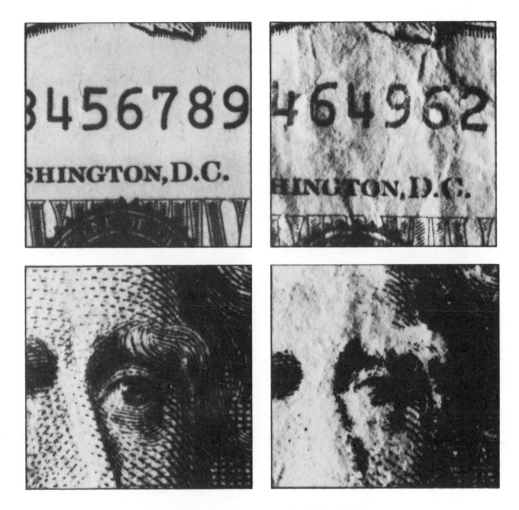

*You can detect a counterfeit bill by looking closely at the portrait on the face or at the border of the bill. The serial numbers of a counterfeit bill may differ in color of ink from the Treasury seal and may not be spaced uniformly.*

Genuine paper money usually looks good. The lines of the engraving are clear and the details of the portrait are sharp. If you think a bill may be counterfeit, check the eyes of the portrait. If the engraving of the eyes is good, chances are that the bill is too. For some reason, the eyes in the portrait are the most difficult feature to copy. Counterfeit money may also look blurry or dull. The Treasury Seal may have broken, uneven or blunt points. The paper may not contain the red and blue threads of real money, or it may have a watermark, which real money never has. The serial number may not be the same color ink as the seal and the numbers themselves may be unevenly spaced.

If you happen to get a counterfeit bill, you should contact your local U.S. Secret Service office, the police, a commercial bank or any Federal Reserve Bank.

# 12　　All About Coin Collecting

Coin collecting, or numismatics, is a fairly new hobby. People have been collecting rare, interesting or old coins for only the last hundred years or so, and it's been only in the last three or four decades that the prices of coins have skyrocketed.

Why do people collect coins? If you asked a dozen collectors why they followed their hobby, you'd get twelve different answers. Most people collect coins because they are beautiful, rare, or valuable. Or the coins may have an interesting story connected with them. There may be a mistake on the coin that makes it one of a kind, or it may be made of an unusual material. Most collected coins are in uncirculated, mint or proof condition.

Some ideas, if you want to start a coin collection, include collecting dimes or quarters dated from before 1964, which are made mostly of silver. These coins are worth more than their face value because of their precious-metal content, and you can still sometimes find them in pocket change—or purchase them from coin dealers at reasonable prices.

Other somewhat common coins worth collecting today include Susan B. Anthony dollars which are unpopular and may be removed from circulation, copper pennies from before 1983, "silver" World War II nickels dated 1942-1945, and zinc pennies from 1943.

You may want to put together a collection of coins and bills dated the same year you were born; try collecting a set for every member of your family. You could find coins with different mint marks, or put together a set of coins from different lands all showing men with beards or women wearing crowns.

Or you may want to collect a full set of Lincoln-head pennies, one for every date printed from 1909 to the present. Or coins that contain mistakes; printed off center or struck twice so that the coin has a double image.

You may want to collect mint proof sets, the special sets of coins made by the U.S. Mint for collectors. These sets include a penny, nickel, dime, quarter, and half-dollar and can be ordered directly from the U.S. Mint or can be found at coin shops. These sets are very popular with serious collectors and tend to sell out every year; and their prices can rise, too.

You can borrow, rent or buy a metal detector and collect the buried coins that you may find. This is a great way to find older coins, or even buried treasure since much pirate booty has never been found and may still be buried. Can you imagine the thrill of finding antique florins, guilders or pieces of eight? It happens!

Now that you've decided to start your coin collection you may be wondering where to keep it. You may want to buy an inexpensive coin-holder book. These books have empty slots for you to pop your coins into; and they also furnish a list of all the dates that the coin you are collecting was minted. They're also a handy way for you to check which coins you still need to complete your collection. The books are inexpensive and can be found in any coin shop.

Once you start a coin collection, it must be properly stored. If you can, keep your coins in a locked desk or dresser drawer. If you do not keep the coins in coin-holder books, store them in paper or cellophane envelopes which are clearly marked with a list of all the coins inside. Or you can roll the coins into paper sleeves which you can get at your local bank.

You may want to start a coin club with your friends or school-mates. The club could go coin hunting together. One idea for your coin club is to have a treasure hunt with a list of coins instead of other objects. For example, a list can ask for a 1968 quarter, a 1982 dime, and a 1955 penny. The first team that finds all the coins on their list would win a small prize such as coin holders or coin books. Your club could report on coin books, take trips to museums to see special coin exhibits or make craft projects with coins. Coin collecting is an easy and fun way to learn about history.

As you begin your coin collection, you'll find it helpful to know some coin collecting terms:

- *Proof:* Struck from special dies and hand polished. These are the best type of coins for collecting.

- *Uncirculated:* Never in general circulation, brand new, but not made with any special handling.

- *Extremely Fine:* Have been in circulation, but are almost like new and are in an unworn condition.

- *Very Fine:* Some wear is shown in spots, especially the higher points of the coin relief, but it generally is in good condition.

- *Fine:* Coins which have been in circulation and show wear. They may have fine scratches or nicks, the finish may be dull, but the words on the coin are all readable.

- *Very Good:* Less good than fine. All the words are readable, but the coin shows more signs of wear and tear.

- *Good:* Definitely a used coin. It may have dents and scratches. All the words on the coin are readable and the worn-down date is clear.

- *Fair:* The words may not be readable since this coin is very worn; the date is clear though.

- *Poor:* The coin is still in existence, but in very bad condition. Unless it's a very rare or valuable coin, it may not be worth more than its face value in this condition.

# Afterword

Now that you have learned all about money and banking and you have become an expert on the subject, you may be interested in learning about a school bank set up in the early 1980s by some sixth graders in Easton, Massachusetts.

These schoolmates lent out as much as $1.50 at a time to cover the cost of forgotten lunch money, for example. They charged 8 percent interest per week on the loans (which comes out to over 400 percent per year.) The bank's customers were other school children.

This school bank experiment was very successful, students repaid their loans and the project was even written about in the national press.

But the bank was shut down by the state bank examiners for operating without a charter (which would have cost $200,000), charging too-high interest rates, using the word bank for a business without permission of the state, and breaking other banking laws. They were allowed to collect their outstanding loans and they then went out of business showing a profit of $46.60. As this book went to press, legislation had just been passed, allowing the bank to reopen.

# Glossary

*Bank*–a business that stores and pays out other people's money. May also offer banking services such as checking and savings accounts, bank credit cards and loans.

*Bank note*–A paper money bill, issued by a bank and backed by the bank.

*Barter*–A system of trading goods or services without the use of money.

*Bill*–Paper money, bank notes.

*Blanks*–Metal disks which are made into coins.

*Bullion*–Gold or silver in the form of bars instead of coins.

*Clipping*–Shaving small bits of precious metal from the edges of coins in circulation.

*Coinage*–Metal, sometimes precious metal, which is stamped with designs by a government, to act as money.

*Consumer*–Someone who uses goods and services and pays for them with cash, barter, checks or credit cards.

*Counterfeit*–Fake money made by someone with the intent of defrauding the government. Counterfeiting money is against the law.

*Currency*–Any kind of money used by a society.

*Denomination*–Amount each piece of currency is worth, usually written out, or in numbers on a coin or paper bill.

*Depression*–An economic condition when many people lose their jobs and there is not very much money being spent.

*Die*–A mold that is used to make coins. Hubs are used to create many dies which are all exactly the same.

*Economy*–The system by which goods and services are produced, distributed, and used.

*Exchange*–to give something for something else thought to be of equal value, such as in barter.

*Financial*–Referring to the management of money and assets.

*Greenbacks*–A nickname for American paper bills.

*Hoarding*–Holding on to a secret supply, sometimes of money, in the fear that it will become scarce.

*Inflation*–An economic condition when there is more money in circulation than there are goods or services to buy. During periods of inflation prices rise.

*Minting*–Making coins.

*Money*–An object, many times a metal coin or paper bill, which is accepted as being valuable by a society, and used for exchange.

*Prime Rate*–The lowest interest rate that the Federal Reserve Banks will give only to their best customers.

*Promissory Note*–A written promise to repay a certain amount of money at a certain time.

*Profit*–Amount of money earned after some kind of uneven exchange.

*Standard value*–A set amount, usually used to measure how much a quantity of money is worth.

*Token*–A piece of stamped metal, used in the place of a coin in certain circumstances.

*Trade*–The exchange of goods and services.

*Value*–The worth of any object, usually measured in money.

# For
# Further
# Reading

Eldred, Pat and Taylor, Paula. *Easy Money Making Projects.* Mankato, Minn.: Creative Education, 1979.

Fodor, R.V. *Nickels, Dimes and Dollars, How Currency Works.* New York: William Morrow and Co., 1980.

Gould, Maurice M. *Gould's Gold and Silver Guide to Coins.* New York: Fleet Press Corp., 1969.

Hobson, Burton H. *Coin Collecting As a Hobby.* New York: Sterling, 1977.

Lewis, Shari. *How Kids Can Really Make Money.* New York: Holt, Rinehart and Winston, 1979.

Reinfeld, Fred. *Treasury of the World's Coins.* New York: Sterling, 1953.

Scott, Elaine. *The Banking Book.* New York: Frederick Warne and Co., 1981.

Seuling, Barbara. *You Can't Count a Billion Dollars & Other Little-Known Facts About Money.* Garden City, New York: Doubleday & Company, 1979.

# Index